" Surely joy is the Condition of life." Henry David Thoreau

Donna Marie Przybyzewski

Henry David Thoreau,

Who Can He Be?

MUSKETAQUID

Read and Find Out – Easy as A,B,C

Written and illustrated by
Donna Marie Przybojewski

StreamlinePUBLISHING

Henry David Thoreau, Who Can He Be?
Read and Find Out–Easy as A, B, C

9 8 7 6 5 4 3 2 1

First Edition
Printed in the United States of America

Library of Congress Control Number: 2016957811
ISBN 978-0-9977851-2-8

Printed on recycled paper

for Henry

> "Every child begins the world again ..."
> Henry David Thoreau, *Walden*

Thank you, Mark, for being the first to read this book to a child, your daughter, Catherine.

Catherine, thank you for telling your daddy not to stop reading it to you.

A is for the **APPLES** under the tree.
Their sweetness alone filled Henry with glee.

B is for Musketaquid, Henry's **BOAT**.
On the Concord River, he loved to float.

C is for Henry's **CABIN** in the wood.
Close to the shore of Walden Pond it stood.

D is for swimming **DUCKS** on Walden Pond.
Of them and the loons, Henry was most fond.

E is for **EMERSON**, mentor and friend.
The land for Henry's cabin he did lend.

F is for the **FISH** Henry held in hand,
scooping them from water where he would stand.

G is for the **GRAPES** that in Concord grew.
A fruit Henry ate – quite more than a few.

H is for the **HAT** Henry always wore.
In it, the plants and flowers he would store.

I is for **ICE** on which Henry would skate.
Leaping and dancing, he never went straight.

J is for the **JOURNALS** that Henry wrote.
Writing daily, much time he would devote.

K is for the Thoreau **KITTEN** named Min.
When it played, Henry would frequently grin.

L is for the **LOVE** of flowers and trees.
Henry loved all nature, including bees.

M is for the sweet **MELONS** Henry grew
and for all the melon parties he threw.

N is for the **NUTS** that Henry would eat.
During his forest walks, they were a treat.

O is for **OCEAN** and its beach of sand.
Henry thought walking at Cape Cod was grand.

P is for the **POPCORN** Henry did make.
The children enjoyed it better than cake.

Q is for **QUIET,** which he loved to be,
for many animals Henry would see.

Ris for the books Henry liked to **READ**.
Throughout his short life, his mind they would feed.

S is for winter's lovely falling **SNOW**.
Henry thought snowflakes made every tree glow.

T is for the large **TURTLE** Henry caught.
"A great reptile to examine," he thought.

U is for the **UMBRELLA** Henry had,
carrying it in case the weather got bad.

V is for **VEGETABLES** Henry ate.
At dinner he would clean them off his plate.

W is for **WALKS** he took daily.
Through the forest Henry sauntered gaily.

X is for E**X**TRAORDINARY man.
Henry David Thoreau, I am his fan.

Y is for **YELLOW** flowers growing wild.
Each time Henry saw them, he always smiled.

Z is for the **ZEST** of living life well.
Therefore, Henry's story is great to tell.

ACKNOWLEDGEMENTS

The Writer's Retreat offered by the Thoreau Farm: Birthplace of Henry David Thoreau in Concord, Massachusetts provides both the amateur and professional writer an opportunity to contemplate, be creative, and pursue literary endeavors. The quiet, rural setting is perfect for anyone who relishes solitude for reflection. Imagine spending time in the very room where Henry David Thoreau was born and being influenced by the ambiance. Imagine writing on a replica of the desk Henry used to write his own drafts.

Margaret Carroll-Bergman, executive director of the Thoreau Farm: Birthplace of Henry David Thoreau, is warm and welcoming to anyone who visits or utilizes the Writer's Retreat as I have. I am deeply indebted to Margaret for offering such a wonderful opportunity to be influenced by the spirit of Henry, and to simply have a place to rest and think without any distractions on the farm where he was born.

During the time I spent at this special place, Margaret made me feel very comfortable. It was at the Writer's Retreat that I was able to initiate my writing. The peaceful atmosphere and solitude inspired me to begin writing books that would introduce Henry David Thoreau to children. This book is one of the products of my time there.

I highly encourage anyone who needs a space for collecting thoughts and pursuing literary tasks to spend a day or more at the Writer's Retreat.

Donna Marie Przybojewski writing on a replica of Henry David Thoreau's desk at the Thoreau Farm: Birthplace of Henry David Thoreau, Writer's Retreat in Concord, Massachusetts.

HENRY DAVID THOREAU

RESOURCES

Concord Museum
53 Cambridge Turnpike
Concord, MA 01742
(978) 369-9763
www.concordmuseum.org

The Old Manse
269 Monument Street
Concord, MA 01742
(978) 369-3909

Ralph Waldo Emerson Memorial House
28 Cambridge Turnpike
Concord, MA 01742

Thoreau Farm:
Birthplace of Henry David Thoreau
341 Virginia Road
Concord, MA 01742
info@thoreaufarm.org

The Thoreau Society
341 Virginia Road
Concord, MA 01742
(978) 369-5310
www.thoreausociety.org

The Thoreau Society Shop at Walden Pond
915 Walden Street
Concord, MA 01742
(978) 287-5477
www.shopatwaldenpond.org